The Ultimate
POCKET POSITIVES

A Second Anthology of Inspirational Thoughts

The Ultimate

POCKET POSITIVES

A Second Anthology of Inspirational Thoughts

Compiled by Maggie Pinkney

THE FIVE MILE PRESS

CONTENTS

You Can Do It!

Opportunities Are for Taking

Light Your Life with Learning

Risk Nothing – Risk Everything!

Defeat Loneliness and Depression

Believe in Miracles

The Joys of Travel

Look to Your Health

Cultivate Contentment

WHAT'S THE USE OF WORRYING?

TAKE COURAGE!

YOU MIGHT AS WELL LAUGH

THE GIFT OF FREEDOM

LET GO OF REGRETS

CALL IT LUCK ...

WHAT IS SUCCESS?

TRY A LITTLE KINDNESS

COMFORTING WORDS

INTRODUCTION

Use the good thoughts of wise people.
Leo Tolstoy, 1828–1910 RUSSIAN WRITER

Good thoughts from the wise abound in this second volume of 'pocket positives'. Open it at any page and you'll find an optimistic, healing or uplifting quotation to brighten your mood.

These wonderful quotations – a distillation of the wisdom of the world's greatest thinkers, poets, writers and leaders – can help you to lead your life to the full. Reflecting on how the thoughts of the wise can make a difference, American actress Helen Hayes wrote, 'We rely on the poets, the philosophers and the playwrights to articulate what most of us can only feel, in joy or sorrow. They illuminate the thoughts for which we can only grope; they give us the strength and balm we cannot find in ourselves…the wisdom of acceptance and the resilience to push on.'

Appreciating the simple things of life, believing in oneself, seizing opportunities when they come up and learning to let go of the past are among the many recurring themes included here. Use this concentration of good thoughts to help you focus on life's positives and to inspire you to greater things.

THE POWER
OF ONE

I am only one. But still I am one.

I cannot do everything, but still I can do something.

I will not refuse to do the something I can do.

Helen Keller, 1880–1968 AMERICAN WRITER AND LECTURER

My will shall shape my future.
Whether I fail or succeed shall be no man's doing but my own.
I am the force. I can clear any obstacle before me or
I can be lost in the maze. My choice, my responsibility.
Win or lose, only I hold the key to my destiny.

Elaine Maxwell AMERICAN WRITER

I believe that we are solely responsible for our choices,

and we have to accept the consequence of every deed,

word and thought throughout our lifetime.

Elisabeth Kübler-Ross, b. 1926 SWISS-BORN AMERICAN PSYCHIATRIST

I don't think of myself as a poor,
deprived ghetto girl who made good.
I think of myself as somebody who from an early age
knew I was responsible for myself,
and I had to make good.

Oprah Winfrey, b. 1954 AMERICAN TELEVISION PERSONALITY

A single hand's turn

given heartily to the world's great work

helps one amazingly

with one's own small tasks.

Louisa May Alcott, 1832–1880 AMERICAN NOVELIST

There is not enough darkness in the world

to extinguish the light

of one small candle.

Spanish proverb

However much I am at the mercy of the world,

I never let myself get lost by brooding over its misery.

I hold firmly to the thought that each one of us can do

a little to bring some portion of that misery to an end.

Albert Schweitzer, 1875–1965 FRENCH PHILOSOPHER AND PHYSICIAN

You can do or be whatever you want in your own life.

Nothing can stop you, except your own fears.

Don't blame anyone else … you have the power

to make the decision. Just do it.

Nola Diamantopoulos GREEK-AUSTRALIAN CREATIVE WORKSHOP TUTOR

There's much to be said

for challenging fate

instead of ducking behind it.

Diana Trilling, 1905–1996 AMERICAN AUTHOR

WHY NOT BE
an OPTIMIST?

I am an optimist.

It does not seem too much use

being anything else.

Sir Winston Churchill, 1874–1965 BRITISH STATESMAN, PRIME MINISTER AND WRITER

All things are possible
until they are proved impossible —
even the impossible may only be so
as of now.

Pearl S. Buck, 1892–1972 AMERICAN WRITER AND MISSIONARY

I have become my own version of an optimist.

If I can't make it through one door,

I'll go through another door — or I'll make a door.

Something terrific will come

no matter how dark the present.

Joan Rivers, b. 1935 AMERICAN COMEDIAN

The very least you can do in your life
is to figure out what you hope for.
And the most you can do is to live inside that hope.
Not admire it from a distance but live right in it,
under its roof.

Barbara Kingsolver, b. 1955 AMERICAN NOVELIST

Optimism is the faith that leads to achievement.

Nothing can be done without hope and confidence.

Helen Keller, 1880–1968 AMERICAN WRITER AND LECTURER

I am an optimist, unrepentant and militant. After all, in order not to be a fool an optimist must know how sad a place the world can be. It is only the pessimist who finds this out anew every day.

Peter Ustinov, b. 1921 ENGLISH WRITER, ACTOR AND DRAMATIST

Expect to have hope rekindled.

Expect your prayers to be answered in wondrous ways.

The dry seasons in life do not last.

The spring rains will come again.

Sarah Ban Breathnach AMERICAN WRITER

Optimists are the elixir of life.

They constantly remind the pessimists that life

isn't as hopeless as they think.

They are the extra ingredient that makes life bubble.

Sara Henderson, b. 1936 AUSTRALIAN OUTBACK STATION MANAGER AND WRITER

The only limit to our realisation of tomorrow

will be our doubts of today.

Let us move forward with strong and active faith.

Franklin D. Roosevelt, 1882–1945 PRESIDENT OF THE UNITED STATES OF AMERICA

*T*omorrow is the most important thing in life.

Comes to us at midnight very clean.

It's perfect when it arrives and it puts itself in our hands.

It hopes we've learnt something from yesterday.

John Wayne, 1907–1979 AMERICAN SCREEN ACTOR

For what human ill does not dawn

seem to be an alleviation?

Thornton Wilder, 1897–1975 AMERICAN WRITER

The optimist is wrong as often as the pessimist.
But he has a lot more fun.

Anonymous

*O*ne of the things I learned the hard way

was that it doesn't pay to get discouraged.

Keeping busy and making optimism a way of life

can restore your faith in yourself.

Lucille Ball, 1911–1989 AMERICAN ACTRESS

DOWN ~ BUT NOT OUT

*O*ur greatest glory is not in never falling,

but in rising every time we fall.

Confucius, c. 550–478 BC CHINESE PHILOSOPHER

My downfall raises me
to great heights.

Napoleon Bonaparte, 1769–1821 FRENCH EMPEROR AND GENERAL

When we begin to take our failures non-seriously,

it means we are ceasing to be afraid of them.

It is of immense importance to learn to laugh at ourselves.

Katherine Mansfield, 1888–1923 NEW ZEALAND WRITER

But what if I fail of my purpose here?

It is but to keep the nerves at a strain,

To dry one's eyes and laugh at a fall,

And, baffled, get up and begin again.

Robert Browning, 1812–1889 ENGLISH POET

He's no failure. He's not dead yet.

Gwilym Lloyd George, 1894–1967 WELSH POLITICIAN

Great works are performed

not by strength

but by perseverance.

Samuel Johnson, 1709–1784 ENGLISH LEXICOGRAPHER, CRITIC AND WRITER

Austere perseverance, harsh and continuous,
may be employed by the smallest of us
and rarely fails its purpose,
for its silent power grows irresistibly
greater with time.

Johann von Goethe, 1749–1832 GERMAN POET AND WRITER

START BY IMAGINING

All the things we achieve

are things we have

first of all imagined.

David Malouf, b. 1934 AUSTRALIAN WRITER

Imagination is the beginning of creation.

You imagine what you desire,

you will what you imagine

and at last you create what you will.

George Bernard Shaw, 1856–1950 IRISH DRAMATIST, WRITER AND CRITIC

*I*magination is the highest kite one can fly.

Lauren Bacall, b. 1924 AMERICAN ACTRESS

Throw your dreams into space like a kite,

and you do not know what it will bring back:

a new life, a new friend,

a new love, a new country.

Anaïs Nin, 1903–1977 FRENCH NOVELIST

Without leaps of imagination, or dreaming,

we lose the excitement of possibilities.

Dreaming, after all, is a form of planning.

Gloria Steinem, b. 1934 AMERICAN FEMINIST AND WRITER

To accomplish great things we must not only act,

but also dream; not only plan, but also believe.

Anatole France, 1844–1924 FRENCH WRITER

Imagination is more important than knowledge.

What is now proved was once only imagined.

William Blake, 1757–1827 ENGLISH POET, ARTIST AND MYSTIC

Imagination finds a road to the realm of the gods,

and there man can glimpse

that which is to be after the soul's liberation

from the world of substance.

Kahlil Gibran, 1883–1931 LEBANESE POET, ARTIST AND MYSTIC

The world is but canvas to our imagination.

Henry David Thoreau, 1817–1862 AMERICAN ESSAYIST AND SOCIAL CRITIC

Knowledge is limited.

Imagination encircles the whole world.

Albert Einstein, 1879–1955 GERMAN-BORN AMERICAN PHYSICIST

SIMPLE PLEASURES

He is happiest, be he king or peasant,

who finds peace in his home.

Johann von Goethe, 1749–1832 GERMAN POET AND WRITER

May I a small house, and large garden have.

And a few Friends, and many Books, both true,

Both wise, and both delightful too.

Abraham Cowley, 1618–1667 ENGLISH POET

The day, water, sun, moon, night —

I do not have to pay to enjoy these things.

Titus Maccius Platus, c. 254–184 BC ROMAN DRAMATIST

I like to walk about among
the beautiful things that adorn the world;
but private wealth *I* should decline,
or any sort of personal possessions,
because they would take away my liberty.

George Santayana, 1863–1952 SPANISH-BORN AMERICAN PHILOSOPHER

If I had two loaves of bread,

I would sell one and buy hyacinths.

For they would feed my soul.

The Qur'an

What a delight it is

When, of a morning,

I get up and go out

To find in full bloom a flower

That yesterday was not there.

Tachibana Akemi, 1812–1868 JAPANESE POET

Yes, in the poor man's garden grow

Far more than herbs and flowers —

Kind thoughts, contentment, peace of mind,

And joy for weary hours.

Mary Howitt, 1799–1888 ENGLISH AUTHOR

Quiet by day,

Sound sleep by night: study and ease

Together mixed; sweet recreation,

And innocence, which most doth please

With meditation.

Alexander Pope, 1688–1744 ENGLISH POET

O gift of God! a perfect day,

Whereon shall no man work but play,

Whereon it is enough for me

Not to be doing but to be.

Henry Wadsworth Longfellow, 1807–1882 AMERICAN POET AND WRITER

One is nearer God's Heart in a garden

Than anywhere else on earth.

Dorothy Frances Gurney, 1858–1932 ENGLISH POET

Who loves a garden still his Eden keeps,

Perennial pleasures, plants and wholesome harvest reaps.

Amos Bronson Alcott, 1799–1888 AMERICAN TEACHER AND PHILOSOPHER

GIVE IT YOUR BEST

Believe in the best, think your best,

study your best, have a goal for your best,

never be satisfied with less than your best, try your best,

and in the long run things will turn out for the best.

Henry Ford, 1863–1947 AMERICAN MOTOR-CAR MANUFACTURER

Good, better, best,

May you never rest,

Until your good is better,

And your better best.

Anonymous

When we do the best we can,

we never know what miracle is wrought in our life

or the life of another.

Helen Keller, 1880–1968 AMERICAN WRITER AND LECTURER

Don't let the best you have done so far

be the standard for the rest of your life.

Gustavus F. Swift, 1839–1903 AMERICAN BUSINESS MAGNATE

There is a better way to do it; find it.

Thomas A Edison, 1847–1931 AMERICAN INVENTOR

I am easily satisfied with the very best.

I do the very best I know how – the very best I can; and I mean to keep on doing it until the end.

Abraham Lincoln, 1809–1865 PRESIDENT OF THE UNITED STATES OF AMERICA

GROWTH ~
AND CHANGE

G rowth, in some curious way, I suspect,

depends on being always in motion just a little bit,

one way or another.

Norman Mailer, b. 1932 AMERICAN WRITER

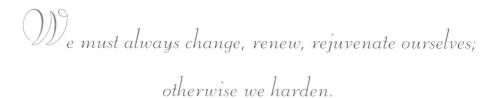

We must always change, renew, rejuvenate ourselves;

otherwise we harden.

Johann von Goethe, 1749–1832 GERMAN POET AND WRITER

Only in growth, reform, and change, paradoxically enough,

is true security to be found.

Anne Morrow Lindbergh, b. 1906 AMERICAN WRITER

Life is change.

Growth is optional.

Choose wisely.

Karen Kaiser Clark, b. 1938 AMERICAN LEGISLATOR AND FEMINIST

We shrink from change;

yet is there anything that can come into being without it?

What does Nature hold dearer, or more proper to herself?

Could you have a hot bath unless the firewood underwent

some change? … Do you not see, then, that change in yourself

is of the same order, and no less necessary to Nature.

Marcus Aurelius, 121–180 AD ROMAN EMPEROR AND PHILOSOPHER

The old woman I shall become

will be quite different from the woman I am now.

Another I is beginning.

Every small positive change we make in ourselves

repays us in confidence in the future.

Alice Walker, b. 1944 AMERICAN AUTHOR

To learn, to desire, to know, to feel, to think, to act.

This is what I want. And nothing else.

That is what I must try for.

Katherine Mansfield, 1888–1923 NEW ZEALAND WRITER

Who is not satisfied with himself will grow.

Hebrew proverb

KEEP YOUR
CURIOSITY ALIVE

A generous and elevated mind

is distinguished by nothing more certainly

than an eminent degree of curiosity.

Samuel Johnson, 1709–1784 ENGLISH LEXICOGRAPHER, CRITIC AND WRITER

Curiosity has its own reason for existing.

Never lose a holy curiosity.

Albert Einstein, 1879–1955 GERMAN-BORN AMERICAN PHYSICIST

Curiosity is a gift, a capacity for pleasure in knowing,

which if you destroy, you make yourselves cold and dull.

John Ruskin, 1819–1900 ENGLISH AUTHOR AND ART CRITIC

Those with a lively sense of curiosity

learn something new every day of their lives.

Anonymous

If I had influence with the good fairy
who is supposed to preside over the christening of all children,
I should ask that her gift to each child in the world
would be a sense of wonder so indestructible
that it would last throughout life.

Rachel Carson, 1907–1964 AMERICAN BIOLOGIST AND WRITER

For a man who cannot wonder

is but a pair of spectacles

behind which there are no eyes.

Thomas Carlyle, 1795–1881 SCOTTISH HISTORIAN, ESSAYIST AND CRITIC

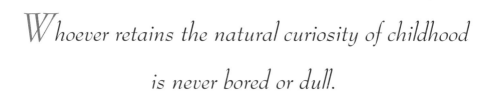

Whoever retains the natural curiosity of childhood

is never bored or dull.

Anonymous

The important thing

is not to stop questioning.

Albert Einstein, 1879–1955 GERMAN-BORN AMERICAN PHYSICIST

Disinterested intellectual curiosity

is the lifeblood of real civilisation.

George Macaulay Trevelyan, 1876–1962 BRITISH HISTORIAN

REFLECTIONS
ON GREATNESS

No great man lives in vain.

The history of the world is but

the biography of great men.

Thomas Carlyle, 1795–1881 SCOTTISH HISTORIAN, ESSAYIST AND CRITIC

I studied the lives of great men and famous women,

and I found the men and women who got to the top

were those who did the jobs they had in hand,

with everything they had of energy and enthusiasm

and hard work.

Harry S. Truman, 1884–1972 PRESIDENT OF THE UNITED STATES OF AMERICA

Great lives never go out.
They go on.

Benjamin Harrison, 1833–1901 PRESIDENT OF THE UNITED STATES OF AMERICA

The heights by great men reached and kept

Were not attained by sudden flight,

But they, while their companions slept,

Were toiling upward in the night.

Henry Wadsworth Longfellow, 1807–1882 AMERICAN POET AND WRITER

*O*ne can build the Empire State Building,
discipline the Prussian army,
make a state hierarchy mightier than God,
yet fail to overcome the unaccountable superiority
of certain human beings.

Alexander Solzhenitsyn, b. 1918 RUSSIAN WRITER

We are all worms, but *I* do believe *I*'m a glow-worm.

Sir Winston Churchill, 1874–1965 BRITISH STATESMAN, PRIME MINISTER AND WRITER

There is a great man,

who makes every man feel small.

But the real great man is the man

who makes every man feel great.

G.K. *Chesterton*, 1874–1936 ENGLISH NOVELIST AND CRITIC

Keep away from people who try to belittle your ambitions.

Small people always do that, but the really great

make you feel that you, too, can become great.

Mark Twain, 1835–1910 AMERICAN HUMORIST AND WRITER

*The measure of a truly great man is
the courtesy with which he treats lesser men.*

Anonymous

Lives of great men all remind us

We can make our lives sublime,

And, departing, leave behind us

Footprints in the sands of time.

Henry Wadsworth Longfellow, 1807–1882 AMERICAN POET AND WRITER

For the courage of greatness is adventurous

and knows not withdrawing,

But grasps the nettle danger, with resolute hands,

And ever again

Gathers security from the sting of pain.

Vera Brittain, 1893–1970 ENGLISH AUTHOR AND POET

Great men are the guide-posts and landmarks in the state.

Edmund Burke, 1729–1797 BRITISH STATESMAN AND PHILOSOPHER

Greatness lies not only in being strong,

but in the right use of strength.

Henry Ward Beecher, 1813–1887 AMERICAN CLERGYMAN

YOU CAN DO IT!

Achievement is largely the product of

steadily raising one's level of

aspiration and expectation.

Jack Nicklaus, b. 1940 AMERICAN GOLFER

If you can walk

You can dance.

If you can talk

You can sing.

Zimbabwean proverb

To achieve great things
we must live as though we were
never going to die.

Luc de Clapiers, Marquis de Vauvenargues, 1715–1747 FRENCH MORALIST AND WRITER

It was a golden year beyond my dreams.

`I proved you're never too old

to achieve what you really want to do.

Heather Turland, b. 1960 AUSTRALIAN WOMEN'S MARATHON GOLD MEDALLIST (Commonwealth Games)

What hat three things do you want to accomplish this year?

Write them down and place them on your refrigerator

for inspiration all year long.

Anonymous

You can have anything you want
if you want it desperately enough.
You must want it with an inner exuberance
that erupts through the skin and joins
the energy that created the world.

Sheilah Graham, 1904–1988 ENGLISH-BORN AMERICAN GOSSIP COLUMNIST

All the strength you need
to achieve anything
is within *you*.

Sara Henderson, b. 1936 AUSTRALIAN OUTBACK STATION MANAGER AND WRITER

OPPORTUNITIES ARE FOR TAKING

Grab a chance
and you won't be sorry for
a might-have-been.

Arthur Ransome, 1884–1967 BRITISH NOVELIST

God helps those that help themselves.

Benjamin Franklin, 1706–1790 AMERICAN STATESMAN AND SCIENTIST

There is no security on this earth;

there is only opportunity.

General Douglas MacArthur, 1880–1964 AMERICAN MILITARY LEADER

There is a tide in the affairs of men
Which, taken at the flood, leads on to fortune;
Omitted, all the voyage of their life
Is bound in shallows and miseries.
On such a full sea we are now afloat,
And we must take the current when it serves,
Or lose our ventures.

William Shakespeare, 1564–1616 ENGLISH POET AND PLAYWRIGHT

A wise man

makes more opportunities

than he finds.

Francis Bacon, 1561–1626 ENGLISH PHILOSOPHER

If your ship doesn't come in,

swim out to it.

Anonymous

Do not wait for extraordinary circumstances to do good;

try to use ordinary situations.

Jean Paul Richter, 1763–1825 GERMAN NOVELIST

Great opportunities to help others seldom come,
but small ones surround us daily.

Sally Koch AMERICAN WRITER

To improve the golden moment of opportunity,

and catch the good that is within our reach,

is the great art of life.

William James, 1842–1910 AMERICAN PSYCHOLOGIST AND PHILOSOPHER

LIGHT YOUR LIFE
WITH LEARNING

Learning should be a joy and full of excitement.

It is life's greatest adventure; it is an illustrated

excursion into the minds of noble and learned men,

not a conducted tour through a jail.

Taylor Caldwell, 1900–1985 AMERICAN WRITER

The primary purpose of a liberal education
is to make one's mind a pleasant place
in which to spend one's leisure.

Sydney J. Harris, b. 1911 AMERICAN JOURNALIST

Learning makes a man fit company for himself.

Thomas Fuller, 1608–1661 ENGLISH DIVINE AND HISTORIAN

K nowledge and understanding

are life's faithful companions who will never be untrue to you.

For knowledge is your crown, and understanding your staff;

and when they are with you, you can possess

no greater treasures.

Kahlil Gibran, 1883–1931 LEBANESE POET, ARTIST AND MYSTIC

If a man empties his purse into his head,
no one can take it from him.

For as the old saying is,

When house and land are gone and spent

Then Learning is most excellent.

Samuel Foote, 1720–1777 ENGLISH ACTOR, DRAMATIST AND WIT

The roots of education are bitter,

but the fruit is sweet.

Aristotle, 384–322 BC GREEK PHILOSOPHER

*T*he supreme end of education is expert discernment in

all things – the power to tell the good from the bad,

the genuine from the counterfeit, and to prefer

the good and genuine to the bad and counterfeit.

Samuel Johnson, 1709–1784 ENGLISH LEXICOGRAPHER, CRITIC AND WRITER

Knowledge is power itself.

Francis Bacon, 1561–1626 ENGLISH PHILOSOPHER AND ESSAYIST

RISK NOTHING ~
RISK EVERYTHING!

Risk! Risk anything!

Care no more for the opinions of others, for those voices.

Do the hardest thing on earth for you. Act for yourself.

Face the truth.

Katherine Mansfield, 1888–1923 NEW ZEALAND WRITER

And the day came when the risk to remain in a tight bud

was more painful than the risk it took to blossom.

Anaïs Nin, 1903–1977 FRENCH NOVELIST

And the trouble is, if you don't risk anything,

you risk even more.

Erica Jong, b. 1942 AMERICAN NOVELIST AND POET

He that is over-cautious will accomplish little.

Friedrich von Schiller, 1759–1805 GERMAN HISTORIAN AND POET

I would not creep along the coast but steer
Out in mid-sea, by guidance of the stars.

George Eliot (Mary Ann Evans), 1819–1880 ENGLISH NOVELIST

*T*ake calculated risks.

This is quite different from being rash.

George S. Patton, 1885–1945 AMERICAN MILITARY LEADER

There are risks and costs to a program of action,
but they are far less than the long-range risks
and costs of comfortable inaction.

John F. Kennedy, 1917–1963 PRESIDENT OF THE UNITED STATES OF AMERICA

A lot of successful people are risk-takers.

Unless you're willing to do that – to have a go,

fail miserably, and have another go,

success won't happen.

Phillip Adams, b. 1939 AUSTRALIAN WRITER AND RADIO BROADCASTER

Take chances, make mistakes. That's how you grow.

Pain nourishes your courage.

You have to fail in order to practise being brave.

Mary Tyler Moore, b. 1937 AMERICAN ACTRESS

Much of the satisfying work of life begins as an experiment; no experiment is ever quite a failure.

Alice Walker, b. 1944 AMERICAN AUTHOR

During the first period of a man's life,

the danger is not to take the risk.

Soren Kierkgaard, 1813–1855 DANISH PHILOSOPHER

No man is worth his salt who is not ready at all times

to risk his body, to risk his well-being,

to risk his life to a great cause.

Theodore Roosevelt, 1858–1919 PRESIDENT OF THE UNITED STATES OF AMERICA

Risk is what separates
the good part of life from the tedium

Jimmy Zero AMERICAN COMEDIAN

DEFEAT LONELINESS AND DEPRESSION

*T*he best remedy for those who are afraid,

lonely or unhappy is to go outside,

somewhere where they can be quite alone

with the heavens, nature and God.

Anne Frank, 1929–1945 DUTCH SCHOOLGIRL DIARIST

If you want people to be glad to meet you,

you must be glad to meet them

— and show it.

Johann von Goethe, 1749–1832 GERMAN POET AND WRITER

That is part of the beauty of all literature.

You discover that your longings are universal longings,

that you're not lonely and isolated from anyone.

You belong.

F. Scott Fitzgerald, 1896–1940 AMERICAN NOVELIST

I will tell you what I have learned for myself.

For me a long, five or six mile walk helps.

And one must go alone and every day.

Brenda Ueland, 1891–1986 AMERICAN WRITER

How to be happy when you are miserable.

Plant Japanese poppies with cornflowers and

mignonette, and set out the petunias among the

sweet-peas so they shall scent each other.

See the sweet-peas coming up.

Rumer Godden, b. 1907 ENGLISH WRITER

$\mathcal{G}$ardening, even if it's only a few pots on a balcony, is a wonderful antidote to anxiety. So, I find, is a long hard walk. And here's a special tip: try finding a place where you can lie on your back and look, for a long time, at the sky. The sky is always there, free for everyone.

Pamela Bone AUSTRALIAN JOURNALIST

It is almost impossible to remember

how tragic a place the world is

when one is playing golf.

Robert Lynd, 1879–1949 IRISH ESSAYIST AND JOURNALIST

*N*oble deeds and hot baths

are the best cures for depression.

Dobie Smith, 1896–1990 ENGLISH WRITER

Drink tea and forget the world's noises.

Chinese saying

The best antidote I have found is to yearn for something. As long as you yearn, you can't congeal: there is a forward motion about yearning.

Gail Godwin, b. 1937 AMERICAN WRITER

Moments of guilt, moments of contrition,

moments when we are lacking in self-esteem,

moments when we are bearing the trial

of being displeasing to ourselves,

are essential to our growth.

M. Scott Peck, b. 1936 AMERICAN PSYCHIATRIST AND WRITER

Whether living alone is adventure or hardship

will depend entirely on your attitude and your decisions.

Become friends with yourself; learn to appreciate who you are

and your unique gifts. Be patient with yourself

and use your sense of humor to keep things in perspective.

Dorothy Edgerton, b. 1911 AMERICAN WRITER

*e gentle with yourself.*

If you will not be your own unconditional friend, who will be?

If you are always playing an opponent and you are also opposing

yourself – you are going to be outnumbered.

Dan Millman AMERICAN WRITER

BELIEVE IN
MIRACLES

Miracles seem to me to rest not so much upon faces

or voices or healing power suddenly near to us from afar off,

but upon our perceptions being made finer, so that

for a moment our eyes can see and our ears can hear

what is there about us always.

Willa Cather, 1876–1947 AMERICAN WRITER

Why, who makes much of a miracle?

As to me I know nothing but miracles —

To me every hour of night and day is a miracle,

Every cubic inch of space a miracle.

Walt Whitman, 1819–1892 AMERICAN POET

I am where I am because I believe in all possibilities.

Whoopi Goldberg, b. 1955 AMERICAN ACTRESS

Miracles are instantaneous;

they cannot be summoned but they come of themselves,

usually at unlikely moments

and to those who least expect them.

Katherine A. Porter, 1890–1980 AMERICAN AUTHOR

Where there is great love,
there are always miracles.

Willa Cather, 1876–1947 AMERICAN WRITER

Increasing success, lasting love and vibrant health

are practical miracles within everyone's reach.

Dr John Grey AMERICAN PSYCHIATRIST AND AUTHOR

Miracles happen to those who believe in them.

Bernard Berenson, 1865–1959 AMERICAN ART CRITIC

THE JOYS OF TRAVEL

Give me the clear blue sky over my head,
and the green turf beneath my feet,
a winding road before me,
and a three hours' march to dinner.

William Hazlitt, 1778–1830 ENGLISH ESSAYIST

A traveler. I love his title.

A traveler is to be reverenced as such.

His profession is the best symbol of life.

Going from – toward; it is the history of every one of us.

Henry David Thoreau, 1817–1862 AMERICAN ESSAYIST AND SOCIAL CRITIC

Traveling and freedom are perfect partners
and offer an opportunity to grow
in new directions.

Donna Goldfein, b. 1933 AMERICAN WRITER

Travel is fatal to prejudice, bigotry and narrow-mindedness.

Mark Twain, 1835–1910 AMERICAN WRITER AND HUMORIST

The wise man travels to discover himself.

James Russell Lowell, 1819-1891 AMERICAN POET AND DIPLOMAT

The soul of a journey is liberty, perfect liberty, to think, feel, do just as one pleases.

William Hazlitt, 1778–1830 ENGLISH ESSAYIST

Keep things on your trip in perspective,
and you'll be amazed at the perspective you gain
on things back home while you're away …
One's little world is put into perspective
by the bigger world out there.

Gail Ruben Bereny, b. 1942 AMERICAN WRITER

For my part,

I travel not to go anywhere, but to go.

I travel for travel's sake.

The great affair is to move.

Robert Louis Stevenson, 1850–1894 SCOTTISH WRITER AND POET

Travel and change of place impart new vigor to the mind.

Seneca, 4 BC–65 AD ROMAN DRAMATIST, PHILOSOPHER AND STATESMAN

LOOK TO
YOUR HEALTH

Look to your health; and if you have it,

praise God, and value it next to a good conscience;

for health is the second blessing that we mortals

are capable of: a blessing that money cannot buy.

Izaak Walton, 1593–1683 ENGLISH WRITER

The preservation of health is a duty.

Few seem conscious that there

is such a thing as physical morality.

Herbert Spencer, 1820–1903 ENGLISH PHILOSOPHER AND JOURNALIST

To wish to be well is part of becoming well.

Seneca, 4 BC–65 AD ROMAN DRAMATIST, PHILOSOPHER AND STATESMAN

O health! health is the blessing of the rich!

the riches of the poor! who can buy thee at too dear a rate,

since there is no enjoying this world without thee?

Ben Jonson, 1573–1637 ENGLISH DRAMATIST AND POET

The Mind is the key to Health and Happiness.

Sai Baba INDIAN SPIRITUAL LEADER

Cheerfulness is the best promoter of health and is as friendly to the mind as to the body.

Joseph Addison, 1672–1719 ENGLISH ESSAYIST

I am convinced digestion is the great secret of life.

Sydney Smith, 1771–1845 ENGLISH CLERGYMAN, ESSAYIST AND WIT

The scientific truth may be put quite briefly:

eat moderately, having an ordinary mixed diet,

and don't worry.

Robert Hutchinson, 1871–1960 BRITISH MEDICAL WRITER

Walking is a man's best medicine.

Hippocrates, c. 460–377 BC GREEK PHYSICIAN

Walking is the best possible exercise.

Habituate yourself to walk very far.

Thomas Jefferson, 1743–1826 PRESIDENT OF THE UNITED STATES OF AMERICA

*Y*our body doesn't lie.

If you listen to it carefully, it will tell you

everything you need to know to keep healthy.

Sara Henderson, b. 1939 AUSTRALIAN OUTBACK STATION MANAGER AND WRITER

The two best physicians of them all —

Dr Laughter and Dr Sleep.

Gregory Dean, 1907–1979 BRITISH PHYSICIAN

To get the body in tone, get the mind in tune.

Zachary T. Berkovitz, 1895–1984 AMERICAN PHYSICIAN AND WRITER

CULTIVATE CONTENTMENT

To live content with small means; to seek elegance rather than luxury; and refinement rather than fashion … to bear all cheerfully, do all bravely, await occasions, hurry never. In a word to let the spiritual, unbidden and unconscious grow up through the common.

This is to be my symphony.

William Ellery Channing, 1780–1842 AMERICAN MINISTER

When we choose not to focus on what is missing from our lives

but are grateful for the abundance that's present — love, health,

family, friends, work, the joys of nature, and personal pursuits

that bring us pleasure — the wasteland of illusion falls away

and we experience heaven on earth.

Sarah Ban Breathnach AMERICAN WRITER

To be content, look backward on those who possess less than yourself, not forward on those who possess more.

Benjamin Franklin, 1706–1790 AMERICAN STATESMAN AND SCIENTIST

A person who is not disturbed by the

incessant flow of desires can alone achieve peace,

and not the man who strives to satisfy such desires.

Bhagavad Gita

*E*verything has its wonders, even darkness and silence,

and I learn, whatever state I'm in, therein to be content.

Helen Keller, 1880–1968 AMERICAN WRITER AND LECTURER

Let us not therefore go hurrying about

and collecting honey, bee-like, buzzing here and there

impatiently from a knowledge of what is to be arrived at.

But let us open our leaves like a flower

and be passive and receptive.

John Keats, 1796–1821 ENGLISH POET

Sweet are the thoughts that savor of content;

The quiet mind is richer than a crown.

Robert Greene, 1558–1592 ENGLISH POET

I am indeed rich, since my income is superior to my expense, and my expense is equal to my wishes.

Edward Gibbon, 1737–1794 ENGLISH HISTORIAN AND WRITER

*H*e is richest who is content with least,

for content is the wealth of nature.

Socrates, 468–399 BC GREEK PHILOSOPHER

WHAT'S THE USE OF WORRYING?

What's the use of worrying?

It never was worthwhile,

So, pack up your troubles in your old kit-bag,

And smile, smile, smile.

George Asaf, 1880–1951 AMERICAN SONGWRITER

I've found that worry and irritation

vanish into thin air the moment I open my mind

to the many blessings I possess.

Dale Carnegie, 1888–1955 AMERICAN MOTIVATIONAL WRITER AND LECTURER

You're only here for a short visit.

Don't hurry. Don't worry.

And be sure to smell the flowers along the way.

Walter C. Hagen, 1892–1969 AMERICAN GOLFER

Leave your worries and shoes outside the door.

Buddhist tradition

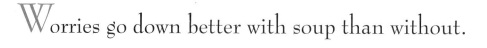

Worries go down better with soup than without.

Jewish proverb

As a cure for worrying,

work is better than whiskey.

Thomas A. Edison, 1845–1931 AMERICAN INVENTOR

The reason why worry kills more people than work
is that more people worry than work.

Robert Frost, 1874–1963 AMERICAN POET

I have spent most of my life worrying about things that never happened.

Mark Twain, 1835–1910 AMERICAN WRITER AND HUMORIST

Why worry? It never gets darker than midnight.

Italian saying

TAKE COURAGE!

You gain strength, courage and confidence

by every experience in which you

really stop to look fear in the face.

You must do the thing you cannot do.

Eleanor Roosevelt, 1884–1962 FIRST LADY OF THE UNITED STATES OF AMERICA, WRITER AND DIPLOMAT

Courage is reckoned the greatest of all virtues,

because, unless a man has that virtue,

he has no security for preserving any other.

Samuel Johnson, 1709–1784 ENGLISH LEXICOGRAPHER, CRITIC AND WRITER

I wanted you to see what real courage is, instead of getting

the idea that courage is a man with a gun in his hand.

It's when you know you're licked before you begin

but you begin anyway and you see it through

no matter what.

Harper Lee, b. 1926 AMERICAN NOVELIST

*M*y message to you is:

Be courageous!

Be as brave as your fathers before you.

Have faith!

Go forward.

Thomas Edison, 1847–1931 AMERICAN INVENTOR

Any coward can fight a battle when he's sure of winning, but give me the man who has pluck to fight when he's sure of losing.

George Eliot (Mary Ann Evans), 1819–1880 ENGLISH NOVELIST

Fearlessness may be a gift, but perhaps more precious is the courage acquired through endeavour, courage that comes from cultivating the habit of refusing to let fear dictate one's actions, courage that could be described as 'grace under pressure' — grace which is renewed repeatedly in the face of harsh, unremitting pressure.

Aung San Suu Kyi, b. 1945 BURMA'S DEMOCRATICALLY ELECTED LEADER AND WINNER OF THE NOBEL PEACE PRIZE

Never bend your head, always hold it high.
Look the world in the face.

Helen Keller, 1880–1968 AMERICAN WRITER AND LECTURER

I am not afraid of storms for I am learning to sail my own ship.

Louisa May Alcott, 1832–1888 AMERICAN NOVELIST

Courage is the price that Life exacts for granting peace.

Amelia Earhart, 1898–1937 AMERICAN PIONEER AVIATOR AND WRITER

You Might as well Laugh

Laughter has something in it in common with the ancient winds of faith and inspiration: it unfreezes pride and unwinds secrecy; it makes men forget themselves in the presence of something greater than themselves; something that they cannot resist.

G.K Chesterton, 1874–1936 ENGLISH NOVELIST AND CRITIC

It's impossible to speak highly enough of the virtues, the dangers and the power of shared laughter.

Françoise Sagan, b. 1935 FRENCH NOVELIST

When you know how to laugh and when to look upon things

as too absurd to take seriously, the other person is ashamed

to carry through even if he was serious about it.

Eleanor Roosevelt, 1884–1962 FIRST LADY OF THE UNITED STATES OF AMERICA, WRITER AND DIPLOMAT

*A*mong those whom I like or admire,

I can find no common denominator,

but among those I love, I can:

all of them make me laugh.

W.H. Auden, 1907–1973 ENGLISH POET

Laughter is sunshine in a house.

William Makepeace Thackeray, 1811–1863 ENGLISH WRITER

Laughter can relieve tension, soothe the pain of

disappointment, and strengthen the spirit for the

formidable tasks that always lie ahead.

Dwight D. Eisenhower, 1890–1969 PRESIDENT OF THE UNITED STATES OF AMERICA

Laughter is a property in man

essential to his reason.

Lewis Carroll, 1832–1898 ENGLISH WRITER, MATHEMATICIAN AND CLERGYMAN

A complete re-evaluation takes place in your physical and mental being when you've laughed and had some fun.

Catherine Ponder AMERICAN MOTIVATIONAL WRITER

Humor is mankind's greatest blessing.

Mark Twain, 1835–1910 AMERICAN WRITER AND HUMORIST

He deserves Paradise who makes his companions laugh.

The Koran

A sense of humor is a sense of proportion.

Kahlil Gibran, 1883–1931 LEBANESE POET, ARTIST AND MYSTIC

THE GIFT
OF FREEDOM

In future days, which we seek to make secure, we look forward to a world founded upon four essential freedoms. The first is the freedom of speech and expression – everywhere in the world. The second is the freedom of every person to worship God in his own way – everywhere in the world. The third is freedom from want … The fourth is freedom from fear.

Franklin D. Roosevelt, 1882–1945 PRESIDENT OF THE UNITED STATES OF AMERICA

Once freedom lights its beacon in a man's heart,

the gods are powerless against him.

Jean-Paul Sartre, 1905–1980 FRENCH WRITER AND PHILOSOPHER

You *only have power over people so long as you don't take*

everything away from them. But when you've robbed a man

of everything he's no longer in your power — he's free again.

Alexander Solzhenitsyn, b. 1918 RUSSIAN WRITER

Freedom's just another word for nothing left to lose.

Kris Kristofferson, b. 1936 AMERICAN ACTOR AND FOLK SINGER

Man is free the moment he wishes to be.

*T*he moment the slave resolves that he

will no longer be a slave, his fetters fall.

He frees himself and shows the way to others.

Freedom and slavery are mental states.

Mahatma Gandhi, 1869–1948 INDIAN LEADER, MORAL TEACHER AND REFORMER

Liberty,

when it begins to take root,

is a plant of rapid growth.

George Washington, 1732–1799 PRESIDENT OF THE UNITED STATES OF AMERICA

LET GO
OF REGRETS

Regret is an appalling waste of energy.

You can't build on it; it is good only for wallowing in.

Katherine Mansfield, 1888–1923 NEW ZEALAND WRITER

Be not like him who sits by his fireside and watches the fire go out, then blows vainly upon the dead ashes. Do not give up hope or yield to despair because of that which is past, for to bewail the irretrievable is the worst of human frailties.

Kahlil Gibran, 1883–1931 LEBANESE POET, ARTIST AND MYSTIC

*T*o regret one's own experiences is to arrest one's own development.

To deny one's own experiences is to put a lie into the lips of

one's own life. It is no less a denial of the soul.

Oscar Wilde, 1854–1900 IRISH POET, WIT AND DRAMATIST

To look up and not down,

To look forward and not back,

To look out and not in –

To lend a hand!

Edward Everett Hale, 1882-1909 AMERICAN UNITARIAN CLERGYMAN AND INSPIRATIONAL WRITER

Nobody gets to live life backward.

Look ahead, that is where your future lies.

Ann Landers, b. 1918 AMERICAN ADVICE COLUMNIST

The past cannot be changed.
The future is yet in your power.

Mary Pickford, 1893–1979 AMERICAN SILENT SCREEN ACTRESS

Make it a rule of life never to regret and never look back.

We all live in suspense, from day to day, from hour to hour;

in other words, we are the hero of our own story.

Mary McCarthy, 1912–1989 AMERICAN AUTHOR AND CRITIC

God grant me the serenity

to accept the things I cannot change,

the courage to change the things I can,

and the wisdom to distinguish

the one from the other.

Reinhold Niebuhr, 1892–1971 AMERICAN THEOLOGIAN

There's no point dwelling on what might or could have been.

You just have to go forward.

Jack Nicholson, b. 1937 AMERICAN ACTOR

CALL IT LUCK ...

I am a great believer in luck,

and I find the harder I work the more I have of it.

Stephen Leacock, 1869–1944 ENGLISH-BORN CANADIAN ECONOMIST AND HUMORIST

I never knew an early-rising, hard-working,

prudent man, careful of his earnings, and strictly honest,

who complained of bad luck.

Joseph Addison, 1672–1719 ENGLISH ESSAYIST AND POLITICIAN

S hallow men believe in luck.

Strong men believe in cause and effect.

Ralph Waldo Emerson, 1803–1882 AMERICAN ESSAYIST AND PHILOSOPHER

How ow can you say luck and chance are the same thing?

Chance is the first step you take, luck is what comes afterwards.

Amy Tan, b. 1952 CHINESE-AMERICAN WRITER

*A*nyone who does not know how to make
the most of his own luck has no right
to complain if it passes him by.

Miguel de Cervantes, 1547–1616 SPANISH WRITER

Luck is infatuated with the efficient.

Persian proverb

Luck to me is something else.

Hard work — and realising what is opportunity and what isn't.

Lucille Ball, 1911–1989 AMERICAN ACTRESS

WHAT IS SUCCESS?

There is only one success — to be able to spend your life in your own way.

Christopher Darlington Morley, 1890–1957 AMERICAN NOVELIST AND ESSAYIST

What's money?

A man is a success if he gets up in the morning and goes to bed at night and in between does when he wants to do.

Bob Dylan, b. 1941 AMERICAN SINGER AND SONGWRITER

There are two kinds of success. One is the very rare kind that comes to the man who has the power to do what no one else has the power to do. That is genius. But the average man who wins what we call success is not a genius. He is a man who has merely the ordinary qualities that he shares with his fellows, but who has developed those ordinary qualities to a more than ordinary degree.

Theodore Roosevelt, 1858–1919 PRESIDENT OF THE UNITED STATES OF AMERICA

Do your work with your whole heart and

you will succeed – there is so little competition.

Elbert Hubbard, 1865–1915 AMERICAN WRITER

I hope I have convinced you – the only thing that separates successful people from the ones who aren't is the willingness to work very, very hard.

Helen Gurley Brown, b. 1922 AMERICAN PUBLISHER AND AUTHOR

One ne only gets to the top rung of the ladder by steadily climbing up,

one at a time, and suddenly all sorts of powers, all sorts of abilities

which you thought never belonged to you — suddenly become within

your own possibility and you think, 'Well, I'll have a go, too'.

Margaret Thatcher, b. 1925 BRITISH PRIME MINISTER

Success is not about money and power. Real success is about relationships. There's no point in making $50 million a year if your teenager thinks you're a jerk and you spend no time with your wife.

Christopher Reeve, b. 1952 AMERICAN SCREEN ACTOR

We are prone to judge success by the index of our salaries

or the size of our automobiles, rather than by the quality

of our service and our relationship to humanity.

Martin Luther King, Jr, 1929–1968 AMERICAN CIVIL RIGHTS LEADER AND MINISTER

Self-trust is the first secret of success.

Ralph Waldo Emerson, 1803–1882 AMERICAN ESSAYIST AND PHILOSOPHER

My mother drew a distinction between achievement and success. She

said that achievement is the knowledge that you have studied and worked

hard and done the best that is in you. Success is being praised by others.

That is nice but not as important or satisfying.

Always aim for achievement and forget about success.

Helen Hayes, 1900–1993 AMERICAN ACTRESS

The secret of success

is making your vocation your vacation.

Mark Twain, 1835–1910 AMERICAN WRITER AND HUMORIST

TRY A LITTLE KINDNESS

No act of kindness,

no matter how small,

is ever wasted.

Aesop, c. 550 BC GREEK FABULIST

*G*uard within yourself that treasure, kindness.

Know how to give without hesitation, how to lose without regret,

how to acquire without meanness …

Know how to replace in your heart, by the happiness of those you love,

the happiness that may be wanting in yourself.

George Sand (Amandine Dupin), 1804–1876 FRENCH NOVELIST

Wise words often fall on barren ground;

but a kind word is never thrown away.

Arthur Helps, 1813–1875 ENGLISH HISTORIAN

The best portion of a man's life,
His little nameless, unremembered acts
of kindness and love.

William Wordsworth, 1770–1850 ENGLISH POET

Little deeds of kindness

Little words of love,

Help to make Earth happy

Like the heaven above.

Julia Fletcher Carney, 1823–1908 AMERICAN EDUCATOR AND POET

One kind word can warm three winters.

Japanese proverb

I expect to pass through this life but once.

If, therefore, there can be any kindness I can show, or any

good thing I can do to any fellow being, let me do it now,

for I shall not return this way again.

William Penn, 1644–1718 ENGLISH QUAKER AND FOUNDER OF PENNSYLVANIA, USA

The heart benevolent and kind

The most resembles God.

Robert Burns, 1759–1796 SCOTTISH POET

So many gods, so many creeds,

So many paths that wind and wind

While just the art of being kind

Is all the sad world needs.

Ella Wheeler Wilcox, 1850–1919 AMERICAN WRITER AND POET

My religion is very simple – my religion is kindness.

Dalai Lama, b. 1945 TIBETAN SPIRITUAL LEADER

Getting money is not all a man's business;
to cultivate kindness is a valuable part of
the business of life.

Samuel Johnson, 1709–1784 ENGLISH LEXICOGRAPHER, CRITIC AND WRITER

When you are kind to someone in trouble,

you hope they'll remember and be kind to someone else.

And it'll become like a wildfire.

Whoopi Goldberg, b. 1955 AMERICAN ACTRESS

Recompense injury with justice,

and recompense kindness with kindness.

Confucius, 551–479 BC CHINESE PHILOSOPHER

Your own soul is nourished when you are kind;

it is destroyed when you are cruel.

Proverbs 11:17

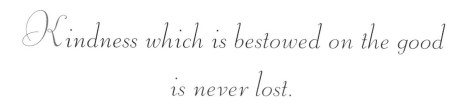

$\mathcal{K}$indness which is bestowed on the good

is never lost.

Plato, 426–c. 347 BC GREEK PHILOSOPHER

COMFORTING WORDS

And this for comfort thou must know:

Times that are ill won't still be so;

Clouds will not ever pour down rain;

A sullen day will clear again.

Robert Herrick, 1591–1674 ENGLISH POET

It is always darkest

just before the day dawneth.

Thomas Fuller, 1608–1661 ENGLISH DIVINE AND HISTORIAN

*W*henever I have found that I have blundered or that my work has been imperfect, and when I have been contemptuously criticised and even when I have been overpraised, so that I have felt mortified, it has been my greatest comfort to say hundreds of times to myself that 'I have worked as hard and as well as I could, and no man can do more than this'.

Charles Darwin, 1809–1882 BRITISH SCIENTIST

And remember, we all stumble, every one of us.

That's why it's a comfort to go hand in hand.

E.K. Brough AMERICAN WRITER

In the midst of winter, I finally learned that there was in me an invincible summer.

For the winter is past, the rain is over and gone.

The flowers are springing up and the time

of the singing of the birds has come.

Yes, Spring is here.

Song of Solomon, 1: 11–12

*E*xpect trouble as an inevitable part of life, and when it comes,

hold your head high, look it squarely in the eye and say,

'I will be bigger than you. You cannot defeat me.'

Then repeat to yourself the most comforting words of all,

'This too will pass'.

Ann Landers, b. 1918 AMERICAN ADVICE COLUMNIST

Master, what is the best way to meet the loss of someone we love?

By knowing that when we truly love, it is never lost.
It is only after death that the depth of the bond is truly felt,
and our loved one becomes more a part of us
than was possible in life.

Oriental tradition

Life is a great surprise.

I do not see why death should not be

an even greater one.

Vladimir Nabokov, 1899–1977 RUSSIAN-BORN AMERICAN NOVELIST

We sometimes congratulate ourselves

at the moment of waking from a troubled dream;

it may be so the moment after death.

Nathaniel Hawthorne, 1804–1864 AMERICAN WRITER

To fear death, gentlemen, is nothing other than to think oneself wise when one is not; for it is to think one knows what one does not know. No man knows whether death may not even turn out to be the greatest of blessings for a human being; and yet people fear it as if they knew for certain that it is the greatest of evils.

Socrates, c. 469–399 BC GREEK PHILOSOPHER

Death is but crossing the world, as friends do the seas; they live on in one another still.

William Penn, 1644–1718 ENGLISH QUAKER AND FOUNDER OF PENNSYLVANIA, USA

The Five Mile Press

The Five Mile Press Pty Ltd
950 Stud Road, Rowville
Victoria 3178 Australia
Phone: +61 3 8756 5500
Email: publishing@fivemile.com.au

First published 2001
Reprinted 2002, 2003, 2004

This compilation © The Five Mile Press Pty Ltd

Editor: Maggie Pinkney
Cover design: Zoë Murphy

Printed in China

National Library of Australia
Cataloguing-in-Publication data

The ultimate pocket positives: a second anthology of inspirational thoughts.

ISBN 1 86503 579 3

1. Quotations, English. 2. Optimism - Quotations, maxims, etc.
3. Success - Quotations, maxims, etc. I. Pinkney, Maggie.
082